THE CROCO SKY SNACK

By Cynthia Rider

Illustrated by John Clementson

CAMBRIDGE
UNIVERSITY PRESS

A crocodile saw a frog going hop.
"Stop!" said the crocodile. "Stop, stop, stop!

I can smash. I can smack. I can snip and snap,
and what I want is a small frog snack."

"Frog snack!" said the frog. "I've got to dash."

So off he swam with a very big splash.

A parrot flew down from the green tree tops.
"Stop!" said the crocodile. "Stop, stop, stop!

I can hit with a stick. I can snip and snap,
and what I want is a small parrot snack."

"Parrot snack!" said the parrot. "I've got to fly."
So off he flew up into the sky.

A snake slid along to a sunny spot.
"Stop!" said the crocodile. "Stop, stop, stop!

I can slam. I can slap. I can snip and snap,
and what I want is a small snake snack."

"Snake snack!" said the snake. "I must slip and slide."
So he slid to a spot where he could hide.

A monkey came along with a skip and a hop.
Then he said to the crocodile, "Just you STOP!

Look at me. I can swing up into the sky.
I can get a big sky snack for you to try."

"This snack looks fresh. This snack looks sweet.
This snack from the sky looks good to eat.

A snack from the sky for me to eat.
Oh my! Oh my! What a snip-snappy treat!"

15

Then the crocodile's jaws went snip and snap,
and he said, "Oh my, what a sweet sky snack!"